Brain Health Easy to Use Guide for Beginners

The Role of Nutrients in Brain Health

By

Phelim Clark

Table of Contents

CHAPTER 1
Introduction

The human brain is a marvel of complexity and sophistication, serving as the command center of our bodies and the epicenter of our thoughts, emotions, and actions. As we embark on a journey to explore the realm of brain health, it becomes clear that our brain's well-being is of paramount importance. This guide, tailored specifically for beginners, aims to shed light on the intricate web of factors that contribute to brain health and underscore its significance in our lives.

1.1 Understanding Brain Health

Before delving into the specifics of brain health, it's crucial to grasp the essence of what it entails. Brain health encompasses the physical, mental, and emotional well-being of the brain. It's not merely the absence of illness but the optimization of brain function to ensure a high quality of life. The brain is an incredibly dynamic organ that constantly changes and adapts, forging new connections and pruning unused ones in a process known as neuroplasticity.

Understanding brain health involves appreciating the brain's incredible versatility. It manages vital bodily functions such as breathing and heart rate, controls our movements, processes sensory input, and enables complex cognitive processes like problem-solving, memory recall, and creative thinking. Moreover, the brain plays a pivotal role in shaping our emotions and reactions, guiding us through the intricate tapestry of human experiences.

As we unravel the layers of brain health, we'll explore the delicate balance between physical, mental, and emotional factors that contribute to its overall well-being. From nourishing our bodies with the right nutrients to engaging in cognitive challenges that keep the mind sharp, every aspect plays a role in shaping our brain's trajectory.

1.2 Importance of Brain Health for Beginners

For beginners, the significance of brain health cannot be overstated. Every individual, regardless of age or background, stands to benefit from nurturing their brain's well-being. A healthy brain lays the foundation for a fulfilling life, enabling us to engage actively with the world around us.

In the early stages of our journey, focusing on brain health can yield lifelong benefits. The habits we establish during this phase can have a profound impact on our cognitive abilities as we age. Just as we care for our bodies through exercise and balanced nutrition, we must extend the same level of care to our brains.

Cultivating good brain health practices can enhance our ability to learn new skills, adapt to changes, and maintain a positive outlook on life. It supports our capacity to handle stress, make sound decisions, and form meaningful relationships. As beginners, we have the opportunity to shape our brain's future by implementing strategies that support its vitality.

In a world where information is constantly at our fingertips, understanding brain health equips us to navigate the digital landscape more effectively. We can learn to strike a balance between technology and genuine human interactions, preventing digital overload and maintaining our cognitive clarity.

The journey to explore brain health as beginners is a transformative one. It empowers us to take proactive steps toward enhancing our overall well-being. By understanding the intricate workings of our brain and its pivotal role in our lives, we can embark on a path that leads to improved cognitive function, emotional resilience, and a richer human experience. So, let us dive into the depths of brain health, armed with the knowledge that each step we take contributes to a brighter and healthier future.

CHAPTER 2

Basics of Brain Function

The human brain, with its intricate network of billions of cells, is the epicenter of human cognition, emotion, and behavior. Here we will unravel the basics of brain function, starting with an exploration of how the brain works, followed by an understanding of neurons and neurotransmitters, and concluding with an examination of the brain's role in our everyday activities.

2.1 How the Brain Works

At the heart of every thought, sensation, and movement lies an intricate dance of electrochemical signals within the brain. The brain's functionality arises from its complex neural network, where billions of specialized cells, called neurons, communicate with one another. Neurons transmit information through electrical impulses and chemical signals, creating a vast and dynamic communication system.

Regions within the brain, each responsible for specific functions, collaborate to produce our conscious experiences. The cerebral cortex, for instance, is responsible for higher-order thinking, language, and sensory processing. The limbic system, on the other hand, influences emotions, motivation, and memory.

The brain's hemispheres, often referred to as the left and right brain, are interconnected by a dense bundle of fibers called the corpus callosum.

This enables information to flow between the two hemispheres, facilitating the integration of logical and creative thinking.

2.2 Neurons and Neurotransmitters

Central to brain function are neurons, the brain's fundamental building blocks. Neurons are specialized cells that process and transmit information. They consist of a cell body, dendrites (which receive signals from other neurons), and an axon (which transmits signals to other neurons). Neurons communicate through synapses, tiny gaps between cells where information is transferred using chemicals known as neurotransmitters.

Neurotransmitters play a crucial role in transmitting signals across synapses. Different neurotransmitters influence various aspects of brain function, such as mood, memory, and cognition. For instance, dopamine is associated with pleasure and reward, while serotonin affects mood and emotional regulation. The balance and interaction of these neurotransmitters are vital for maintaining optimal brain function and mental well-being.

2.3 Brain's Role in Everyday Activities

The brain's influence extends far beyond complex thoughts and emotions—it's integral to our daily activities. Simple actions like walking, talking, and eating involve multiple brain regions working in harmony. For example, motor cortex areas coordinate muscle movements, while sensory areas process the information received from our senses.

Beyond the basics, the brain also shapes our responses to the environment. The amygdala, a key component of the limbic system, plays a pivotal role in processing emotions, especially fear and anxiety. In contrast, the prefrontal cortex is involved in decision-making, problem-solving, and impulse control.

The brain's role in everyday activities extends to learning and memory as well. As we encounter new information, the brain's hippocampus and other memory-related regions encode and store these experiences. When we recall information, various brain regions collaborate to retrieve and reconstruct memories.

The brain's functioning is an intricate symphony of neurons, neurotransmitters, and specialized regions. Understanding the basics of brain function helps us appreciate the complexity underlying even the simplest of activities. As we delve deeper into the realms of brain health, this knowledge serves as a foundation to make informed decisions and engage in practices that promote optimal brain function and overall well-being.

CHAPTER 3
Factors Affecting Brain Health

Brain health is intricately connected to various lifestyle factors that can significantly impact cognitive function, emotional well-being, and overall mental vitality.

3.1 Diet and Nutrition

The saying "you are what you eat" holds profound truth when it comes to brain health. The brain is a metabolically active organ that requires a constant supply of nutrients to function optimally. A well-balanced diet rich in essential nutrients supports cognitive function, memory, mood regulation, and overall brain vitality.

Omega-3 fatty acids, found in fatty fish like salmon and walnuts, play a crucial role in brain health by supporting neural communication and reducing inflammation. Antioxidant-rich foods such as berries, dark leafy greens, and colorful vegetables help protect brain cells from oxidative stress. B-vitamins, present in whole grains, eggs, and legumes, are essential for energy production and neurotransmitter synthesis.

Conversely, a diet high in saturated fats, refined sugars, and processed foods can have detrimental effects on brain health. Such diets have been linked to cognitive decline and an increased risk of neurodegenerative diseases like Alzheimer's.

Maintaining proper hydration is also essential, as even mild dehydration can impair cognitive function and focus. Additionally, incorporating brain-boosting foods like turmeric (rich in curcumin, known for its anti-inflammatory properties) and nuts (a source of healthy fats and antioxidants) can contribute to long-term brain health.

3.2 Physical Exercise and Brain Health

The adage "a healthy body leads to a healthy mind" holds true in the context of brain health. Regular physical exercise has far-reaching positive effects on the brain. Engaging in aerobic activities like walking, running, or swimming increases blood flow to the brain, delivering oxygen and nutrients that support its function.

Exercise triggers the release of chemicals like endorphins, often referred to as "feel-good" hormones, which enhance mood and reduce stress. Moreover, exercise stimulates the production of brain-derived neurotrophic factor (BDNF), a protein that supports the growth and maintenance of neurons, aiding in learning and memory.

Physical activity is also associated with improved cognitive function and a reduced risk of cognitive decline with aging. It enhances neuroplasticity, the brain's ability to reorganize and form new connections in response to learning and experiences.

Incorporating regular exercise into your routine doesn't have to be complicated. Even moderate activities like brisk walking, yoga, or dancing can contribute to improved brain health. The key is consistency, as the cumulative effects of physical activity over time yield significant benefits for both body and mind.

Both diet and physical exercise play pivotal roles in shaping brain health. By nourishing the brain with the right nutrients and engaging in regular physical activity, you can foster an environment that supports cognitive function, emotional well-being, and overall brain vitality. These lifestyle factors, when approached with intention and commitment, lay the groundwork for a resilient and thriving brain throughout your life.

3.3 Sleep and its Impact on the Brain

Sleep is often underestimated in its significance for overall health and brain function. It's during sleep that the brain performs crucial maintenance and repair processes, consolidates memories, and rejuvenates for the day ahead.

Quality sleep is essential for cognitive functions such as attention, problem-solving, and decision-making. During the various stages of sleep, the brain cleanses itself of waste products that accumulate throughout the day. This process, known as the glymphatic system, helps prevent the buildup of harmful substances that could potentially contribute to neurodegenerative diseases.

Moreover, sleep plays a pivotal role in memory consolidation. The brain processes and organizes information gathered during waking hours, transferring it from short-term to long-term memory storage. REM (rapid eye movement) sleep, a stage of sleep associated with vivid dreaming, is particularly important for this memory-related function.

Disrupted sleep patterns or chronic sleep deprivation can have detrimental effects on cognitive function. It can lead to difficulties in concentration, mood disturbances, and impaired decision-making. Over time, inadequate sleep has been linked to an increased risk of cognitive decline, Alzheimer's disease, and other neurological disorders.

To promote healthy sleep habits, establish a consistent sleep schedule, create a comfortable sleep environment, and prioritize relaxation techniques before bedtime. Limiting screen time and caffeine intake close to bedtime can also contribute to better sleep quality.

3.4 Stress Management for Brain Health

Stress is an inevitable part of life, but chronic and unmanaged stress can have negative implications for brain health. The brain's response to stress involves the release of stress hormones like cortisol, which, in excess, can impair cognitive function and contribute to mood disorders.

Chronic stress has been associated with structural changes in the brain, particularly in areas involved in memory and emotional regulation. It can also lead to inflammation, which has been linked to a range of neurological conditions.

Effective stress management is crucial for preserving brain health. Techniques like mindfulness meditation, deep breathing exercises, and yoga can help reduce stress and promote relaxation. Engaging in hobbies, spending time in nature, and maintaining social connections are also effective ways to alleviate stress and improve overall well-being.

Furthermore, a balanced lifestyle that includes regular physical activity and a healthy diet can buffer the effects of stress on the brain. Adequate sleep also plays a vital role in stress management, as sleep deprivation can amplify the body's stress response.

Incorporating stress-reduction practices into your daily routine can have a positive impact on brain health, enhancing cognitive function, emotional resilience, and overall quality of life. By recognizing the importance of stress management and implementing strategies that work for you, you're taking proactive steps to support your brain's well-being.

sleep and stress management are two critical factors that influence brain health. Prioritizing restorative sleep and adopting effective stress reduction techniques can contribute to optimal cognitive function, emotional well-being, and the long-term vitality of your brain. By nurturing these aspects of your lifestyle, you're investing in a healthier and more vibrant brain for the future.

CHAPTER 4

Mental Stimulation and Cognitive Activities

Engaging your brain through mental stimulation and cognitive activities is akin to exercise for your mind. Just as physical activity keeps your body fit, challenging your brain keeps your cognitive abilities sharp and enhances overall brain health.

4.1 Importance of Mental Stimulation

The brain thrives on novelty and complexity. Mental stimulation involves exposing your brain to new experiences, ideas, and challenges that require active thinking. Just as physical exercise strengthens muscles, mental stimulation strengthens neural connections and encourages the growth of new ones. This process is crucial for maintaining cognitive function and preventing cognitive decline.

Regular mental stimulation can enhance memory, problem-solving skills, and creativity. It can also help build cognitive reserve—the brain's ability to adapt and function effectively even in the face of age-related changes or neurological damage.

4.2 Brain-Boosting Games and Puzzles

Engaging in brain-boosting games and puzzles is an enjoyable and effective way to challenge your mind. Activities like crossword puzzles, Sudoku, and logic games stimulate different cognitive functions, including language, memory, and critical thinking.

These games encourage you to think in new ways, make connections between different pieces of information, and develop strategies to solve problems. Regularly engaging in such activities can improve cognitive flexibility—the ability to switch between different tasks and adapt to changing situations.

Digital platforms offer a wide range of brain-training apps and games designed to target specific cognitive skills. While these can be entertaining, it's also important to incorporate a variety of cognitive challenges beyond the digital realm.

4.3 Learning a New Skill for Brain Health

Learning a new skill is an incredibly effective way to promote brain health and neuroplasticity—the brain's ability to reorganize and adapt by forming new neural connections. Whether it's playing a musical instrument, learning a new language, or acquiring a craft, the process of learning activates various areas of the brain and encourages growth.

Learning a new skill involves stepping out of your comfort zone, making mistakes, and persisting through challenges. This process not only stimulates your brain but also fosters a sense of accomplishment and self-confidence.

Additionally, learning a new skill can have positive effects on other areas of your life. It can enhance your creativity, boost your problem-solving abilities, and improve your overall cognitive function.

mental stimulation through brain-boosting activities and learning new skills is a cornerstone of brain health. Just as you would engage in physical exercise to keep your body in shape, engaging your mind through various challenges keeps your brain agile and resilient. By incorporating cognitive activities and embracing opportunities

to learn and grow, you're investing in
a future of enhanced cognitive
function and a richer intellectual
experience.

CHAPTER 5

Social Connections and Brain Health

Human beings are inherently social creatures, and our interactions with others have a profound impact on our mental and emotional well-being.

5.1 Social Interaction's Effect on the Brain

Social interactions are not only integral to our emotional experiences but also play a pivotal role in shaping the structure and function of the brain. The brain is highly attuned to social cues, and our interactions trigger a cascade of neurochemical responses that influence our thoughts, emotions, and behavior.

When we engage in positive social interactions, the brain releases oxytocin, often referred to as the "bonding hormone." Oxytocin promotes feelings of trust, empathy, and connection, fostering social cohesion and a sense of belonging. These interactions activate reward pathways in the brain, leading to feelings of pleasure and reinforcing our desire to connect with others.

Conversely, social isolation or loneliness can have detrimental effects on brain health. Chronic loneliness is associated with increased levels of stress hormones and inflammation, both of which can negatively impact brain function. It can also lead to a heightened risk of mental health issues, such as depression and anxiety.

Engaging in meaningful social interactions can have a range of cognitive benefits. Conversations stimulate various brain regions responsible for language processing, comprehension, and emotional understanding. Engaging with diverse perspectives challenges our cognitive biases and encourages flexible thinking.

Moreover, maintaining social connections as we age is linked to better cognitive outcomes. Interacting with others provides mental stimulation, keeps the mind engaged, and may even slow down age-related cognitive decline.

social interactions have a profound impact on brain health. Positive social connections contribute to emotional well-being, release neurochemicals that foster social bonding, and stimulate brain regions responsible for cognitive processes. Prioritizing social engagement and fostering strong relationships is a crucial aspect of maintaining optimal brain health throughout life.

5.2 Building and Maintaining Relationships

Building and maintaining relationships is not only essential for our emotional and social well-being but also has a significant impact on our brain health. Meaningful connections with others contribute to a sense of belonging, support, and fulfillment, all of which play a vital role in promoting optimal brain function. In this section, we'll delve into the importance of building and nurturing relationships for brain health.

Cognitive Stimulation Through Interactions: Engaging in conversations and interactions with others provides cognitive stimulation that keeps the brain active and engaged. Meaningful discussions require us to process information, recall memories, and formulate responses, all of which exercise different cognitive functions. Whether it's discussing current events, sharing personal experiences, or debating ideas, these interactions contribute to cognitive flexibility and mental agility.

Emotional Support and Stress Reduction: Strong relationships provide emotional support that can buffer the effects of stress. Sharing our thoughts, concerns, and emotions with trusted individuals can have a calming effect on the brain. Positive social interactions trigger the release of oxytocin, promoting feelings of well-being and reducing stress hormones like cortisol. Having a support system can help us navigate life's challenges with resilience, preventing the negative impact of chronic stress on brain health.

Neuroplasticity and Learning: Engaging with diverse individuals exposes us to different perspectives, cultures, and ideas. This exposure encourages neuroplasticity—the brain's ability to reorganize and adapt. Learning from others, hearing their stories, and engaging in open discussions stimulate neural connections and promote cognitive growth. The brain remains receptive to new information and experiences, contributing to ongoing cognitive vitality.

Preventing Isolation and Loneliness: Social isolation and loneliness have been linked to a range of negative health outcomes, including cognitive decline and depression. Building and maintaining relationships help prevent feelings of loneliness by fostering a sense of belonging and companionship. Being part of a social network provides opportunities for engagement, laughter, and shared experiences that contribute to overall well-being.

Tips for Building and Nurturing Relationships:

1. **Initiate Communication:** Reach out to friends, family, or acquaintances to start conversations and foster connections.

2. **Active Listening:** Show genuine interest in others by actively listening to their stories and perspectives.

3. **Shared Activities:** Engage in shared activities or hobbies that provide opportunities for interaction and bonding.

4. **Quality Time:** Dedicate quality time to spend with loved ones, whether it's in person or through virtual platforms.

5. **Express Gratitude:** Express appreciation and gratitude for the relationships in your life, reinforcing positive connections.

6. **Open Communication:** Foster open and honest communication, allowing for meaningful discussions and deeper connections.

7. **Volunteer or Join Groups:** Participate in community activities, clubs, or volunteer opportunities to meet new people and expand your social circle.

Building and maintaining relationships is a powerful way to promote brain health. Meaningful social connections provide cognitive stimulation, emotional support, and opportunities for learning and growth. By prioritizing the cultivation of strong relationships, you're nurturing your brain's well-being and enriching your overall quality of life.

CHAPTER 6

Lifestyle Habits for Optimal Brain Health

Our daily lifestyle choices have a profound impact on the health and vitality of our brain. By adopting habits that prioritize brain well-being, we can enhance cognitive function, emotional resilience, and overall mental clarity.

6.1 Mindfulness and Meditation

In a world filled with constant distractions and information overload, the practice of mindfulness and meditation offers a sanctuary for the brain. Mindfulness is the practice of being fully present in the moment, cultivating awareness of your thoughts, emotions, and sensations without judgment. Meditation, a closely related practice, involves intentional focus and can take various forms, such as focused attention or loving-kindness meditation.

Benefits for Brain Health:

1. **Stress Reduction:** Mindfulness and meditation are renowned for their ability to reduce stress and anxiety. These practices activate the relaxation response, calming the nervous system and lowering levels of stress hormones.

2. **Emotional Regulation:** By observing your thoughts and

emotions without attaching judgment, you develop greater emotional self-regulation. This allows you to respond to situations with clarity rather than reacting impulsively.

3. **Improved Focus and Attention:** Regular meditation enhances attention and concentration. The practice of focusing on your breath or a specific object trains the brain to sustain attention and resist distractions.

4. **Enhanced Cognitive Function:** Mindfulness and meditation have been associated with improved cognitive function, including better memory, problem-solving, and decision-making abilities.

5. **Neuroplasticity:** These practices encourage neuroplasticity—the

brain's ability to rewire itself. By focusing attention and cultivating awareness, you strengthen neural connections and promote the growth of new ones.

Incorporating Mindfulness and Meditation:

1. **Start Small:** Begin with short sessions of 5-10 minutes and gradually extend the duration as your practice deepens.

2. **Choose a Comfortable Space:** Find a quiet and comfortable place where you can sit or lie down without distractions.

3. **Focus on the Breath:** A common meditation technique involves focusing on your breath. Observe the sensation of each inhale and exhale.

4. **Non-Judgmental Awareness:** As thoughts arise, acknowledge them without judgment and gently return your focus to your breath or chosen point of attention.

5. **Guided Sessions:** Consider using guided meditation apps or online resources to help structure your practice.

6. **Consistency is Key:** Consistency is more important than duration. Aim for daily practice, even if it's just for a few minutes.

Incorporating mindfulness and meditation into your daily routine, you're cultivating a space of mental clarity, emotional balance, and cognitive vitality. These practices offer a sanctuary for the brain in the midst of a busy world, allowing you to tap into your inner resources for optimal brain health.

6.2 Balancing Work and Leisure

Our daily choices play a crucial role in maintaining brain health. Striking a balance between work and leisure is essential for promoting cognitive function, reducing stress, and fostering overall well-being.

In today's fast-paced world, the line between work and personal time can become blurred, leading to increased stress and reduced brain health. Achieving a balance between these two aspects of life is essential for several reasons:

Stress Reduction and Mental Resilience: Balancing work and leisure helps prevent burnout and chronic stress. Engaging in leisure activities provides an opportunity to relax, unwind, and recharge. By giving your brain time to rest and rejuvenate, you enhance your mental resilience and reduce the negative impact of stress on cognitive function.

Cognitive Performance and Creativity: Engaging in leisure activities unrelated to work can boost cognitive performance. These activities allow your brain to shift its focus and engage in different thought processes. Such mental flexibility can enhance problem-solving skills, creativity, and innovation.

Emotional Well-Being: Leisure activities often bring joy and pleasure. Participating in hobbies, spending time with loved ones, or simply taking a leisurely stroll can release dopamine—the "feel-good" neurotransmitter—promoting emotional well-being and a positive outlook on life.

Quality of Relationships: Balancing work and leisure ensures that you have time for meaningful interactions with friends and family. Strong social connections are vital for brain health, and spending quality time with loved ones provides emotional support and enhances cognitive stimulation.

Tips for Balancing Work and Leisure:

1. **Set Boundaries:** Establish clear boundaries between work and personal time. Avoid checking work emails during leisure hours and designate specific times for relaxation.

2. **Prioritize Leisure:** Treat leisure activities as non-negotiable appointments. Schedule them in your calendar just like you would work commitments.

3. **Disconnect:** Make a conscious effort to disconnect from digital devices during leisure time. This minimizes distractions and allows you to fully engage in the present moment.

4. **Engage in Varied Activities:** Pursue a diverse range of leisure activities that bring you joy, whether it's reading, hiking, painting, or dancing.

5. **Practice Mindfulness:** When engaging in leisure activities, practice mindfulness by fully immersing yourself in the

experience and savoring each moment.

6. **Delegate and Manage Time:** Delegate tasks when possible and manage your time effectively to prevent work from spilling into leisure hours.

Finding the right balance between work and leisure is a dynamic process that requires conscious effort and regular adjustments. Prioritizing leisure time not only benefits your brain health but also enhances your overall quality of life. By nurturing both professional and personal aspects of your life, you create a harmonious environment that supports cognitive vitality and emotional well-being.

6.3 Avoiding Harmful Substances

Maintaining brain health requires mindful choices in various aspects of our lives. One critical factor is avoiding harmful substances that can negatively impact cognitive function, emotional well-being, and overall brain vitality.

Certain substances can have detrimental effects on the brain's structure and function. It's crucial to be aware of these substances and make informed choices to safeguard your brain health.

Alcohol: Excessive alcohol consumption can impair cognitive function and memory. Chronic alcohol use can lead to conditions like alcohol-related dementia, which affects memory, attention, and decision-making. Limiting alcohol intake and avoiding binge drinking is essential for maintaining optimal brain health.

Tobacco and Nicotine: Smoking tobacco or using nicotine products harms the brain's blood vessels and increases the risk of stroke. Nicotine addiction can also lead to cognitive impairments and negatively impact memory and concentration. Quitting smoking and avoiding nicotine products contribute to better brain health.

Recreational Drugs: Many recreational drugs, such as cocaine, methamphetamine, and ecstasy, can damage brain cells, alter neurotransmitter levels, and impair cognitive function. Prolonged use can lead to addiction and severe cognitive deficits. Avoiding recreational drug use is crucial for preserving brain health.

Prescription and Over-the-Counter Medications: Some medications, including certain sleep aids, antianxiety drugs, and anticholinergic drugs, can have cognitive side effects, especially in older adults. It's important to discuss potential cognitive effects with your healthcare provider and explore alternative medications if necessary.

Processed Foods and Artificial Additives: Diets high in processed foods, artificial additives, and excessive sugars can lead to inflammation and oxidative stress, both of which can negatively impact brain health. Opt for a balanced diet rich in whole foods, fruits, vegetables, and healthy fats to support brain vitality.

Chronic Stress and Overwork: While not substances in the traditional sense, chronic stress and overwork can have harmful effects on the brain. Prolonged stress increases cortisol levels, which can damage brain cells and impair cognitive function. Prioritizing stress management and work-life balance is essential for brain health.

Sleep Disruption: Inadequate sleep or poor sleep quality can disrupt cognitive function, memory consolidation, and emotional regulation. Avoid habits that interfere with sleep, such as excessive caffeine consumption or irregular sleep patterns.

Avoiding harmful substances is a critical component of maintaining optimal brain health. By making informed choices and prioritizing your brain's well-being, you're taking steps to ensure that your cognitive function, emotional resilience, and overall quality of life remain intact. Remember that your brain's health is a reflection of the cumulative impact of your lifestyle choices, and each decision you make contributes to its vitality.

CHAPTER 7

Brain-Boosting Foods and Nutrients

The old saying "you are what you eat" holds a profound truth when it comes to brain health. The foods we consume play a crucial role in shaping our cognitive function, mood, and overall brain vitality.

7.1 The Role of Nutrients in Brain Health

The brain is a highly metabolically active organ that requires a constant supply of nutrients to function optimally. Nutrients are the building blocks that support neural communication, energy production, and various biochemical processes within the brain. Here are some key nutrients that contribute to brain health:

1. **Omega-3 Fatty Acids:** Found in fatty fish (such as salmon, mackerel, and sardines), flaxseeds, and walnuts, omega-3 fatty acids are crucial for brain health. They support the structure of brain cell membranes, promote neuroplasticity, and have anti-inflammatory properties that protect against cognitive decline.

2. **Antioxidants:** Vitamins like vitamin C and E, as well as compounds like flavonoids and polyphenols found in fruits, vegetables, and tea, act as antioxidants. They help protect brain cells from oxidative stress,

reducing the risk of
neurodegenerative diseases.

3. **B Vitamins:** B vitamins, including
   B6, B12, and folate, are essential
   for energy production and
   neurotransmitter synthesis. These
   vitamins can be found in whole
   grains, leafy greens, eggs, and lean
   meats.

4. **Choline:** Choline, found in eggs,
   liver, and soybeans, is a precursor
   to acetylcholine—a
   neurotransmitter crucial for
   memory and learning.

5. **Iron:** Iron is necessary for
   delivering oxygen to the brain.
   Sources of iron include lean meats,
   beans, and fortified cereals.

6. **Magnesium:** Magnesium supports
   brain function by regulating
   neurotransmitter release and

promoting relaxation. It can be found in nuts, seeds, whole grains, and leafy greens.

7. **Zinc:** Zinc is involved in neural communication and plays a role in memory and learning. Foods rich in zinc include seafood, meat, and legumes.

8. **Protein:** Protein provides amino acids necessary for building neurotransmitters that regulate mood and cognitive function. Lean sources of protein like poultry, fish, and beans are beneficial.

9. **Carbohydrates:** The brain relies on glucose for energy. Choosing complex carbohydrates like whole grains, fruits, and vegetables ensures a steady supply of energy to the brain.

10. **Hydration:** Staying adequately hydrated is crucial for cognitive function. Dehydration can impair concentration, memory, and decision-making.

It's important to maintain a balanced diet that includes a variety of nutrient-rich foods to support brain health. Incorporating a colorful array of fruits and vegetables, healthy fats, lean proteins, and whole grains can provide the essential nutrients that contribute to optimal cognitive function and overall well-being.

The nutrients we consume have a direct impact on brain health. By making conscious choices to include brain-boosting foods in your diet, you're providing your brain with the nourishment it needs to function at its best. A balanced and nutrient-rich diet is a powerful way to invest in your cognitive vitality and long-term brain health.

7.2 Omega-3 Fatty Acids and Brain Health

Omega-3 fatty acids are a class of essential polyunsaturated fats that play a crucial role in brain health and function. fats are not produced by the body, so they must be obtained through dietary sources.

Omega-3 fatty acids are known for their neuroprotective properties, benefiting the brain in various ways:

1. Cognitive Function and Memory: Omega-3 fatty acids, particularly a specific type known as docosahexaenoic acid (DHA), are abundant in the brain and essential for cognitive function. DHA is a key structural component of brain cell membranes, influencing cell fluidity and communication. Adequate levels of DHA are associated with improved cognitive performance, memory, and learning.

2. Neuroplasticity and Mood Regulation: Omega-3s support neuroplasticity—the brain's ability to adapt and reorganize itself. They enhance the growth of new neurons and synapses, particularly in regions associated with memory and emotion regulation. Research suggests that omega-3 fatty acids may play a role in reducing the risk of mood disorders such as depression and anxiety.

3. Anti-Inflammatory Effects: Chronic inflammation is linked to cognitive decline and neurodegenerative diseases. Omega-3s have anti-inflammatory properties that help protect brain cells from damage and support overall brain health.

4. Neurological Disorders: Omega-3 fatty acids have been studied for their potential benefits in preventing or managing neurological disorders such as Alzheimer's disease and Parkinson's disease. While more research is needed, these fatty acids show promise in reducing cognitive decline and supporting brain function.

Sources of Omega-3 Fatty Acids:

1. **Fatty Fish:** Fatty fish like salmon, mackerel, sardines, and trout are excellent sources of omega-3s, particularly DHA and EPA (eicosapentaenoic acid).

2. **Flaxseeds:** Flaxseeds and flaxseed oil contain alpha-linolenic acid (ALA), a type of omega-3 fatty

acid. ALA can be converted into DHA and EPA in the body, although the conversion rate is limited.

3. **Chia Seeds:** Chia seeds are another plant-based source of ALA.

4. **Walnuts:** Walnuts are rich in ALA and offer a convenient way to incorporate omega-3s into your diet.

5. **Seaweed and Algal Oil:** Some algal sources and seaweed-based products provide a vegan-friendly source of DHA and EPA.

Incorporating Omega-3s into Your Diet:

To support brain health, aim to include omega-3-rich foods in your diet regularly. Fatty fish can be a staple in your meals, and you can also sprinkle flaxseeds or chia seeds on cereals, yogurt, or smoothies. If you have dietary restrictions or preferences, algal oil supplements can provide a source of DHA and EPA.

omega-3 fatty acids are essential for optimal brain health. By including omega-3-rich foods in your diet, you're providing your brain with the necessary building blocks for cognitive function, memory, and emotional well-being. As part of a balanced diet, omega-3s contribute to your brain's resilience and long-term vitality.

7.3 Antioxidants and Their Benefits

Antioxidants are powerful compounds found in various foods that help protect our cells from oxidative stress and damage caused by harmful molecules called free radicals. Oxidative stress is associated with numerous health conditions, including cognitive decline and neurodegenerative diseases.

Antioxidants play a vital role in maintaining brain health by neutralizing free radicals and reducing oxidative stress. Here's how they benefit the brain:

1. Protection Against Oxidative Damage: Oxidative stress occurs when there's an imbalance between free radicals and antioxidants in the body. Free radicals are highly reactive molecules that can damage cells, including brain cells. Antioxidants neutralize free radicals, preventing their harmful effects and reducing the risk of cellular damage.

2. Preserving Cognitive Function: Oxidative stress contributes to age-related cognitive decline and neurodegenerative diseases such as Alzheimer's and Parkinson's. Antioxidants help protect brain cells from damage, preserving cognitive function and potentially reducing the risk of these diseases.

3. Supporting Neuroplasticity: Antioxidants promote neuroplasticity—the brain's ability to reorganize and form new connections. By reducing oxidative stress, antioxidants create a favorable environment for learning, memory, and adaptability.

4. Reducing Inflammation:
Inflammation is linked to many brain disorders. Some antioxidants have anti-inflammatory properties that can help mitigate neuroinflammation, a factor in conditions like depression and Alzheimer's disease.

5. Enhancing Mood and Well-Being: Antioxidants can positively influence mood and emotional well-being. Some studies suggest that a diet rich in antioxidants is associated with a reduced risk of depression and improved mental well-being.

Sources of Antioxidants:

1. **Colorful Fruits and Vegetables:** Brightly colored fruits and vegetables such as berries, oranges, spinach, kale, and peppers are rich in antioxidants like

vitamin C, vitamin E, and flavonoids.

2. **Nuts and Seeds:** Almonds, walnuts, and sunflower seeds contain vitamin E, which is a potent antioxidant.

3. **Dark Chocolate:** Dark chocolate is rich in flavonoids, particularly cocoa polyphenols, which have antioxidant and anti-inflammatory effects.

4. **Tea:** Green tea and black tea contain polyphenols, including catechins, which have antioxidant properties.

5. **Spices:** Herbs and spices like turmeric, cinnamon, and ginger are high in antioxidants that can support brain health.

6. **Omega-3 Fatty Acids:** As mentioned earlier, omega-3 fatty acids also have antioxidant properties that contribute to brain health.

Incorporating Antioxidants into Your Diet:

Aim to include a variety of colorful fruits and vegetables in your diet to ensure a diverse range of antioxidants. Snacking on nuts and seeds, enjoying a square of dark chocolate, and sipping on antioxidant-rich tea are also delicious ways to enhance your brain health.

antioxidants are key players in promoting brain health. By consuming a diet rich in antioxidant-containing foods, you're providing your brain with the tools it needs to fend off oxidative stress and maintain optimal cognitive function. A rainbow-colored plate is a simple yet effective strategy for nurturing your brain's resilience and overall well-being.

CHAPTER 8

Creating a Brain-Healthy Environment

Our surroundings have a significant impact on our overall well-being, including brain health. Organizing your living space in a way that promotes relaxation, focus, and positive emotions can contribute to optimal cognitive function and emotional balance.

8.1 Organizing Your Living Space

A cluttered and disorganized living space can have negative effects on your mental and emotional well-being, including increased stress and decreased productivity. Creating an organized and harmonious environment, on the other hand, can provide several brain-boosting benefits:

1. Reduced Stress: A clutter-free environment can help reduce stress levels. Visual clutter and chaos can overwhelm the brain, triggering the release of stress hormones. An organized space promotes a sense of calm and relaxation.

2. Enhanced Focus: A tidy and organized space minimizes distractions and makes it easier for your brain to focus. When your environment is free from clutter, your mind can concentrate more effectively on the task at hand.

3. Improved Productivity: An organized space enhances productivity by allowing you to locate items easily and move through tasks without unnecessary disruptions. This efficiency can positively impact your cognitive function and sense of accomplishment.

4. Positive Mood: A clean and orderly living space can have a positive impact on your mood. Surrounding yourself with a visually pleasing environment can trigger the release of dopamine, the brain's "feel-good" neurotransmitter.

5. Better Sleep: A bedroom that is clutter-free and designed for relaxation can contribute to better sleep quality. A calming environment promotes restful sleep, which is essential for brain health.

Tips for Organizing Your Living Space:

1. **Declutter Regularly:** Set aside time to declutter and organize different areas of your living space. Donate or discard items you no longer need or use.

2. **Designate Storage Spaces:** Assign specific places for items to prevent clutter from accumulating. Use storage solutions that suit your needs, such as shelves, bins, and drawers.

3. **Create Zones:** Designate different areas for specific activities. For example, have a dedicated

workspace, a reading nook, and an area for relaxation.

4. **Minimize Visual Clutter:** Keep surfaces clear of unnecessary items. Use minimal decor and choose a simple color palette to create a visually soothing atmosphere.

5. **Prioritize Comfort:** Arrange furniture in a way that promotes comfort and flow. Ensure that seating and workspaces are ergonomically designed.

6. **Personalize Your Space:** Incorporate elements that bring you joy, such as plants, artwork, or photos. These personal touches contribute to a positive and welcoming environment.

7. **Regular Maintenance:** Keep up with the organization by tidying up

daily or weekly. This prevents clutter from accumulating and overwhelming your space.

Creating an organized and harmonious living space is an investment in your brain health and overall well-being. By surrounding yourself with an environment that supports relaxation, focus, and positivity, you're creating the conditions for optimal cognitive function and emotional balance.

8.2 Incorporating Nature and Natural Light

The connection between our environment and brain health extends to our relationship with nature and exposure to natural light. Both elements have a profound impact on cognitive function, mood regulation, and overall well-being.

1. Benefits of Nature:

Stress Reduction: Spending time in natural environments has been shown to lower cortisol levels, reducing stress and promoting relaxation. Natural settings offer a sanctuary for the brain, allowing it to unwind and recharge.

Mood Enhancement: Exposure to nature can elevate mood and trigger the release of endorphins—the brain's natural "feel-good" chemicals. Nature's beauty and tranquility have a positive impact on emotional well-being.

Cognitive Restoration: Natural settings provide a respite from the mental fatigue caused by daily tasks and technology use. Time spent in nature allows the brain to recover and rejuvenate, enhancing cognitive function.

2. Benefits of Natural Light:

Regulation of Circadian Rhythms: Natural light helps regulate the body's internal clock, known as the circadian rhythm. Exposure to natural light during the day and reduced exposure in the evening supports healthy sleep-wake cycles and overall well-being.

Mood Enhancement: Natural light triggers the release of serotonin—a neurotransmitter associated with mood regulation and a sense of well-being. Sunlight exposure can alleviate symptoms of seasonal affective disorder (SAD) and boost overall mood.

Cognitive Performance: Natural light has been linked to improved cognitive performance, including enhanced focus, attention, and alertness. It can positively impact productivity and cognitive function.

Tips for Incorporating Nature and Natural Light:

1. **Maximize Window Access:** Arrange your living space to allow natural light to flow in. Position furniture and workspaces near windows to benefit from sunlight exposure.

2. **Use Nature-Inspired Decor:** Incorporate elements of nature into your decor, such as plants, natural materials, and artwork depicting landscapes or natural scenes.

3. **Create a Green Space:** If possible, introduce indoor plants into your living space. Plants not

only improve air quality but also provide a connection to nature.

4. **Spend Time Outdoors:** Whenever possible, spend time outdoors in natural environments. Whether it's a walk in the park, a hike, or simply sitting in your garden, exposure to nature has numerous benefits.

5. **Choose Natural Materials:** opt for natural materials in your furniture and decor. Wood, stone, and natural textiles can contribute to a calming and nature-inspired atmosphere.

6. **Open Curtains and Blinds:** During daylight hours, open curtains and blinds to allow natural light to fill your living space.

7. **Consider Light Quality:** Pay attention to the quality of artificial

lighting as well. Choose warm, white light that mimics natural sunlight for a more inviting and calming atmosphere.

Creating an environment that integrates nature and natural light can positively influence your brain health and overall well-being. By incorporating elements of the natural world into your living space, you're creating a haven for relaxation, cognitive vitality, and emotional balance.

8.3 Minimizing Digital Overload

In our modern world, the constant presence of digital devices and screens can have a significant impact on brain health. Managing your digital environment and reducing digital overload is crucial for maintaining cognitive function, managing stress, and promoting overall well-being.

1. Cognitive Overload: The constant influx of information from digital devices can lead to cognitive overload, making it difficult for the brain to process and retain information effectively. This can lead to decreased attention span and reduced cognitive performance.

2. Disrupted Sleep: Exposure to screens, especially before bedtime, can interfere with the body's production of melatonin—a hormone that regulates sleep. This can disrupt sleep patterns and negatively impact cognitive function the next day.

3. Increased Stress: Constant notifications, emails, and the pressure to stay connected can contribute to chronic stress. High stress levels can impair cognitive function and overall brain health.

4. Reduced Face-to-Face Interaction: Excessive screen time can lead to reduced face-to-face social interactions, which are vital for brain health. In-person interactions stimulate areas of the brain responsible for emotional understanding, empathy, and communication.

5. Blue Light Exposure: The blue light emitted by screens can suppress the production of melatonin and disrupt sleep-wake cycles. It can also contribute to eye strain and fatigue.

**Tips for Minimizing Digital
Overload:**

1. **Set Boundaries:** Establish specific
   times for checking emails and
   social media. Create digital-free
   zones in your home, such as the
   bedroom or dining area.

2. **Practice Digital Detox:** Dedicate
   regular periods of time without
   screens. Disconnecting from
   digital devices can help your brain
   reset and recharge.

3. **Prioritize Quality Content:** Be
   selective about the content you
   consume. Focus on high-quality
   information and limit mindless
   scrolling.

4. **Use Screen Filters:** Use blue light
   filters on your devices, especially
   during the evening. These filters

reduce blue light exposure and promote better sleep.

5. **Unplug Before Bed:** Avoid screens at least an hour before bedtime to promote healthy sleep patterns.

6. **Engage in Offline Activities:** Dedicate time to activities that don't involve screens, such as reading a physical book, practicing a hobby, or spending time in nature.

7. **Digital Declutter:** Regularly declutter your digital devices by deleting unnecessary apps, emails, and files. A clean digital space can reduce mental clutter.

8. **Set Notifications:** Disable non-essential notifications to reduce distractions and the constant urge to check your devices.

9. **Practice Mindfulness:** Practice mindful technology use by being fully present when engaging with digital devices. Avoid multitasking and focus on one task at a time.

creating boundaries around digital use and prioritizing face-to-face interactions and offline activities, you can minimize digital overload and promote brain health. Striking a balance between digital engagement and unplugged time is essential for maintaining cognitive clarity, emotional well-being, and overall quality of life.

CHAPTER 9

Recognizing Warning Signs and Seeking Help

9.1 Common Brain Health Concerns

Monitoring your brain health and recognizing potential warning signs is essential for early intervention and effective management of any concerns. While everyone's brain health journey is unique, there are common concerns that you should be aware of:

Memory Changes: Noticeable changes in memory, particularly short-term memory loss, could be indicative of underlying issues such as mild cognitive impairment or dementia.

Mood Disorders: Frequent mood swings, persistent feelings of sadness or hopelessness, and changes in behavior or social withdrawal might suggest mood disorders like depression or anxiety.

Cognitive Decline: Difficulties with concentration, decision-making, problem-solving, or experiencing confusion might be early signs of cognitive decline or neurodegenerative conditions.

Sleep Disturbances: Chronic sleep disturbances, including insomnia or excessive sleepiness, can impact brain health and cognitive function.

Headaches: Frequent or severe headaches could indicate various issues, including migraines, tension headaches, or other underlying conditions.

Vision Changes: Sudden or significant changes in vision could point to neurological or eye-related concerns that warrant investigation.

Movement Issues: Tremors, unexplained coordination problems, or other movement-related issues could signal neurological conditions such as Parkinson's disease.

When to Consult a Healthcare Professional

Persistent Symptoms: If you notice persistent changes in cognitive function, mood, behavior, or physical health, it's important to consult a healthcare professional.

Worsening Symptoms: If symptoms worsen over time or interfere with daily activities, seeking medical guidance is crucial.

Concerns About Memory: If you or a loved one experience memory problems that are impacting daily life, consider seeking a medical evaluation.

New or Unexplained Symptoms: The sudden onset of new or unexplained symptoms, such as severe headaches or vision changes, requires prompt medical attention.

Family History: If you have a family history of neurological conditions or cognitive decline, it's important to stay vigilant and consult a healthcare professional if you notice any concerning changes.

Overall Decline in Function: If you observe a decline in overall functioning, such as difficulty managing daily tasks, it's important to address this with a healthcare provider.

Regular Check-ups: Even in the absence of noticeable symptoms, regular check-ups with a healthcare provider can help monitor your brain health and address any concerns early on.

seeking help and early intervention are crucial for managing brain health concerns. Healthcare professionals can provide accurate diagnoses, guidance, and recommendations for treatment or lifestyle adjustments that can positively impact your brain health and overall well-being.

9.2 Committing to Long-Term Brain Health

Maintaining brain health is a lifelong commitment that involves consistent efforts and mindful choices. By prioritizing your brain health, you're investing in your cognitive vitality, emotional well-being, and overall quality of life.

Benefits of Long-Term Commitment:

1. **Cognitive Resilience:** A sustained commitment to brain health can help build cognitive resilience, allowing your brain to adapt to changes and challenges over time.

2. **Reduced Risk of Cognitive Decline:** Engaging in brain-boosting activities, maintaining a healthy lifestyle, and seeking

timely medical attention can
reduce the risk of cognitive decline
and neurodegenerative diseases.

3. **Enhanced Emotional Well-Being:** Prioritizing brain health can lead to improved mood, better stress management, and greater emotional resilience.

4. **Optimal Quality of Life:** A healthy brain supports your ability to engage in meaningful activities, maintain relationships, and pursue your interests throughout life.

9.3 Your Personal Brain Health Action Plan

Creating a personalized action plan for brain health empowers you to make informed decisions and cultivate habits that support cognitive well-being. Here's how to create your own action plan:

1. Assess Your Current Habits: Take stock of your current lifestyle habits, including diet, physical activity, sleep, stress management, and screen time. Identify areas that might need improvement.

2. Set Specific Goals: Set realistic and specific goals for improving your brain health. For example, you could aim to engage in regular physical exercise, incorporate more brain-boosting foods into your diet, or establish a consistent sleep routine.

3. Prioritize Brain-Boosting Activities: Choose activities that challenge your brain, such as puzzles, learning a new instrument, or taking up a new hobby. Schedule regular time for these activities.

4. Plan Healthy Nutrition: Design a balanced diet rich in brain-boosting nutrients. Incorporate omega-3 fatty acids, antioxidants, and whole foods while minimizing processed foods and excessive sugars.

5. Cultivate Emotional Well-Being: Practice stress reduction techniques, mindfulness, and relaxation exercises to support emotional well-being.

6. Stay Socially Engaged: Prioritize meaningful social interactions to foster strong social connections, which contribute to brain health.

7. Limit Screen Time: Set boundaries around digital device use to prevent digital overload and promote healthy sleep patterns.

8. Regular Check-ups: Schedule regular check-ups with healthcare professionals to monitor your brain health, especially if you have concerns or a family history of neurological conditions.

9. Stay Curious and Engaged: Continuously seek out new learning opportunities, experiences, and challenges to keep your brain engaged and active.

10. Celebrate Progress: Regularly review your action plan, celebrate your achievements, and make adjustments as needed.

Creating a brain health action plan is a powerful step toward ensuring long-term cognitive vitality. By committing to your plan and making conscious choices that prioritize brain health, you're setting the stage for a vibrant and fulfilling life. Remember that small, consistent actions over time can have a profound impact on your brain's well-being and your overall quality of life.